BYGONE

of

Longbenton, Benton, Forest Hall, West Moor and Killingworth.

by

W.G. Elliott and Edwin Smith.

Published by W.G. Elliott.

Acknowledgements.

The authors would like to thank all those listed below for providing historical information and/or photographs. If we have inadvertently omitted anyone, then please accept our apologies.

Newcastle upon Tyne City Library * (both Local Studies and Publications Dept).
North Shields Public Library* (Local Studies - Mr. Eric Hollerton).
Northumberland County Archives Department, Melton Park, Gosforth.
Northumberland County History Committee. (use of History of Northumberland. Vol 13 by M.H. Dodds).
The Ordnance Survey.

Mr. H.W. Burchell.	Mr. J.C. Dean.*	Mr. A. Oliver.*	Mr. T.H. Rowland.
Mrs. M. Burchell.*	Mr. H. Hutchinson.*	Mr. J.M. Potts.*	Mr. R. Thompson.
Mrs. J.D. Clasper.*	Mrs. D. Hutchinson.*	Mr. N.K. Punshon.*	Mrs. M. Welsh.*

Permission to use postcards and photographs are shown *.

Published by: - W.G. Elliott.

Copyright © W.G. Elliott and Edwin Smith.

ISBN: 0 9535633 0 8

Distributed to the trade by Publications, Newcastle Libraries & Information Service, City Library, Princess Square, Newcastle upon Tyne, NE99 1DX. Tel: 0191 2610691, Fax: 0191 2612911 and North Tyneside Libraries, Northumberland Square, North Shields, Tyne and Wear, NE30 1QU. Tel: 0191 2005424. Fax: 0191 2006118.

Printed by Pattison and Sons, 94-102 Blandford Street, Newcastle upon Tyne NE1 3BT. Telephone: (0191) 232 0379. Fax: (0191) 261 0854

INTRODUCTION.

It was during my research for historical detail to contribute towards the booklet to mark the Centenary of The Grove, Benton in 1995, that I realised that there was no collection of material available covering the local area. Newcastle Libraries' 'Bygone' series has produced many booklets covering the various suburbs of Newcastle upon Tyne, but none had produced material covering the bygone days of Longbenton, Benton, Forest Hall, West Moor and Killingworth. This booklet is therefore an attempt to remedy this situation.

Having moved into Westcroft Road, Forest Hall in 1927, where my family home had remained until 1984 and living in The Grove, Benton for the past 36 years, I feel reasonably qualified to attempt this task.

Along with Mr. Edwin Smith of High Heaton, who has very strong family links with the old village of Longbenton, going back some 175 years or more and armed with only a selection of his vast array of old photographs, books and maps, we commence our journey. This takes the form of a perambulation from the Four Lane Ends, Longbenton, through the old village of Longbenton, down past Benton Station and then on to old Forest Hall. Reaching Clousden Hill, we turn westwards along Great Lime Road, passing through West Moor and then retrace our steps, turning into West Lane to finally reach the old village of Killingworth.

Unfortunately the cost of space precludes us from including many views and old maps but we hope that the enclosed portrays a memorable record of the past.

Armed with this booklet, you should be able to imagine the bygone days of the area, going back over 200 years in some places. Be prepared for some surprises and do not delay, as several old properties are under threat of demolition as we go to press.

WGE.

EARLY HISTORY OF THE AREA.

de Merley

Sommerville

ap Griffyth

Thornton

Heron

Brandling

Stote

Dorothy Windsor

Wilson

Reay

Bell

Early History of the Parish of Longbenton.

The Manor was held under the Barony of Merley (or Morpeth) dating from the beginning of the 12th century.

Roger de Merley III died 1265/6 leaving three daughters.
Alice died young and the barony was divided between the survivors, Mary and Isobel - subject to the life interest of Margery, daughter of Richard of Umfraville and widow of Roger de Merley II, to whom on her later marriage to John of Lexington, her son Roger III had granted the manors of Ulgham, Longbenton and Killingworth and the advowson* of the church of Longbenton for life.

Mary married William, baron of Greystoke (see later page).

Isobel married Robert de Sommerville and in
1298   as his widow, granted her purparty ** of the barony, including the manor of Witton and a moiety # of the manor of Benton with the advowsons* of Benton and Stannington, to her younger son Roger de Sommerville, even though her heir was an older son, Edmund, who did not die until c.1318, when Roger Sommerville became his heir.

1310   Longbenton Church mentioned as being dedicated to St. Andrew. (Cal Pat R. 1307-13. p. 294).

1337   Roger died - heir was his younger brother Philip aged 50.

1339/40   Philip granted to Balliol College the advowson and two cottages and land called 'The Buttes' to sustain six scholars and a chaplain.

*   advowson - right of presentation to a benefice.
**   purparty   - a proportion, a share, especially in an inheritance.
#   moiety   - usually half, but can be any equal share.

(At this time patronage of the church, which was dedicated to St. Andrew, was transferred to Balliol College, Oxford.
 It is interesting to note that the advowson remains with the College to the present day).

Church appropriated by Royal Licence.
20s. annually reserved to the Bishop of Durham.
10s. "   "   " Prior and Convent.
Annuity of 35 marks to John de Sommerville the last rector.

<u>Endowment of vicarage:</u> -   The Glebe.
                                Small tithes.
                                Easter Offerings.
                                Payments for - Baptisms.
                                                Marriages.
                                                Burials.
(Tithes commuted 1843).

1340   Philip granted his moieties of Benton and Stannington to Rhys ap Griffyth (son-in-law) and daughter Joan - perhaps in revenge for a serious quarrel which he had with his other son-in-law John Stafford.

1355   Philip died leaving as heirs

        Joan   Elizabeth dvd
        m. Rhys de Griffyth.   m. John de Stafford.

                                              Maud m. Edmund de Vernon.

Despite the grant to the Griffyths in 1340, Longbenton was nevertheless divided between the co-heiresses, as on -

10th May.
1356   Rhys ap Griffyth (Snr) died seised of a quarter of the manor of Longbenton held in right of his wife Joan who survived him - his heir being his son Rhys ap Griffyth (Jnr) aged 30.

1371 Rhys (Jnr) granted all his Northumberland lands to his brother Henry ap Griffyth and Joan his wife.

1372   Sir Henry died - succeeded by his daughter Margaret in 1387 (aged 17). She was granted as ward to John de Neville and married William de Carnaby.

1379   Edmund Vernon died seised of the other quarter of Longbenton in right of his late wife Maud. Maud did not have any children so Rhys (Jnr) was heir and the two quarters were united. Later that same year, Rhys died leaving a son and heir Thomas ap Griffyth - aged 3.

1387   Margaret died without children, her heir being her cousin Thomas ap Griffyth whose wardship was granted to John de Neville who had also been ward to Margaret.

1405/6 Thomas sold his Northumberland properties including the Sommerville moiety of Longbenton to Roger Thornton.

1430   Roger Thornton died leaving his estates to his son Roger Thornton II, who settled his moiety with Coldcoats and Witton on the Water, on his illegitimate sons and property descended upon the issue of John Thornton, the third of these sons.

18th April.
1532   John's son and heir Nicholas died, his heir being his son - another Roger aged 18.

1570   This Roger settled his half of Longbenton upon marriage of his daughter Marion with Thomas Heron of Crawley in Eglingham parish, by Catherine his wife. The family was descended from John Heron the Bastard, illegitimate elder brother of William Heron of Ford.

1582   Thomas Heron died leaving three daughters, Margaret and Barbara and an unborn child. If this child were a boy, his father willed that he should be heir to all his lands 'except that at Longbenton which my daughter Margaret must have'. If this child were a girl, she was to share equally with her sisters. (His mother Catherine was to have a life interest in 1/3rd of Crawley). He named as guardians of his three children 'My cousyn Henry Anderson, my cousyn Henry Mitford and my cousyn Henry Chapman - now Sherife of Newcastle.'

The child proved to be a boy as in ...

1586　John, son and heir of Thomas Heron, is entered as a freeholder in Crawley.

1654　Next mention of this Sommerville moiety when it is the property of Sir Francis Brandling...and Sir Francis being dead:
Sir Nicholas Tempest }
Thomas Wraye   } Executors
Francis Anderson   }
Sold this part of Longbenton to Richard Stote of Lincoln's Inn, in discharge of Sir Francis Brandling's debts.

1682　Sir Richard Stote died.

1707　His son and heir Bertram died d.s.p. leaving as co-heiresses his three sisters:
Margaret Tonge
Frances Shippen
Dorothy was the last survivor and she had married the Hon. Dixie Windsor, the third son of the last Earl of Plymouth.

1731　Part of her land at Longbenton (known as Forest Hall) was bought by Richard Wilson.

1746　Wilson mortgaged some of the land to George Cuthbertson of Newcastle for £600.

1752　Further mortgage for £400

1756　Dorothy died intestate and without issue and the estates were claimed and possessed by Sir Robert Bewick of Close House, Wylam and John Craster of Craster as rightful heirs, being descendents of Dorothy Windsor's great-great-grandfather. Their claim was challenged by the Crown and others, but after litigation, was finally settled in their favour in 1857. (+Richardson p.62).

　+The History of the Parish of Wallsend - William Richardson. Published 1923.

1799 The mortgages of 1746 and 1752 were never redeemed and following deaths and much litigation, a Report of the Master of the Rolls said that the estates involved were to be sold. Henry Utrick Reay of Killingworth bought some of the land, which he gave to his daughter as dowry on her marriage to Matthew Bell of Woolsington Hall and Sheriff of Northumberland, later to become M.P. for Northumberland in 1816. The Bells had no children and the land passed to one of the sons of the second brother, Henry Bell. Bell thus obtained about half of the Wilson estate.

Returning to the other half of Roger de Merley III's land at Longbenton which descended to his other daughter Mary...
Mary married William, Baron of Greystoke.
In C.15 Greystoke heiress married a Dacre of Naworth.
In C.16 three Dacre heiresses were betrothed to three Howard sons: younger brothers of the Duke of Norfolk.
Elizabeth Dacre married Lord William Howard.

In 1661 their great grandson was created:
    1). Baron Dacre of Gilsland.
    2). Viscount Morpeth.
    3). Earl of Carlisle.

We thus have Earls of Carlisle as Lords of the Manor of Longbenton, until 1802 when they sold their part of the barony to Charles Brandling and William Brown.

It has been said that this part of the estate had remained in direct descent for six hundred years.

WGE.

THE GROWTH OF LONGBENTON VILLAGE.

Longbenton, formerly Benton Magna (sometimes appearing as Mickle Benton or Gret Benton) can be found down to the sixteenth century, frequently spelt BEMPTON. From medieval times, the parish boundary embraced the five townships of Weetslade, Killingworth, Longbenton, Little Benton and Walker. However, these boundaries changed during the last century.

Longbenton developed as a linear village on a desolate moor approximately 60 metres above sea level. The dominant building was the Church of St. Andrew (later becoming St. Bartholomew's Parish Church) which was situated to the north of the village and which dates back to 820AD.

An early map of village garths dated 1755, shows public houses on the sites of both the Sun Inn and the Black Bull, traditionally the oldest pub in Longbenton. During the eighteenth and nineteenth centuries, wealthy mine owners built their mansions in and around Longbenton from stone quarried locally. These included Benton Lodge, Benton Grange, Benton Park, Benton Hall, Forest Hall and Killingworth House. However the only survivor of these great houses is Benton House, built by the Bigges of Bigges Main in the 1740's. In more recent years, Benton House became the Clubhouse of the Benton Golf Club and now belongs to the Conservative Club.

Around 1791, the village of Longbenton consisted of one street of small cottages, occupied by farm workers, pitmen and other traders. Some wealthy farmers also served the village and many provided agricultural services such as blacksmiths, herdsmen, joiners and knifesharpeners.

There were also many lawyers who had come to the area in the seventeenth century, no doubt attracted by rumours of wealth to be made from the growing coal trade. They married into local families such as the Dents and Hindmarshes, whose daughters brought coal-bearing land as dowries and thus established the business interests of the Bigges of Benton, Wallsend and Willington.

The Earls of Carlisle had also worked some coal pits in the area but in 1802, following what we would now call 'a rationalisation of their interests', the Carlisles sold their Longbenton estate. It was bought by the Brandlings, who were then living at Gosforth Park and the Browns who were later to buy the Bigges' house at Benton.

At that time, the Brandlings were well-established industrial merchants, particularly in the coal trade. The Browns had more modest connections, originally at pits in the Throckley area but they were to play an important part in the growing local industry. Bell's Coal Royalties map of 1847 shows how extensive were the areas they controlled, and, of course, the employment they offered in the area.

The Tithe map of 1842 (and a section is printed overleaf), shows that the Brandlings held 690 acres, the Duke of Northumberland 367 acres, Balliol 320 acres, the Browns 261 acres, F.W. Wilson of the Hall, Forest Hall 154 acres and the vicar's Glebe 84 acres.

The enlarged section which follows, shows clearly the make-up of the early settlement in Longbenton in 1842 and the following key identifies the main dwellings and occupants. It is noted that what is now Station Road, formed a route at this time and is likely to have determined the location of early building in this area. The only other buildings on this large map are Longbenton Church, The Hall, Forest Hall, Benton North Farm, Wagon Man's Row and East Benton Farm.

The earliest Ordnance Survey map dated 1858 (revised in 1894) still shows Longbenton as a small compact village. Billy Pit (previously known as the William Pit) and the Richard Pit are prominent with Benton Quarry in full service. (Benton West Quarry had become disused in the latter years). To the west lies the North Eastern railway with a station at Forest Hall. This line is crossed overhead at right angles near the last named Quarry by the Blyth and Tyne railway. (Now the Metro line). Near this junction stands Swiss Villa, Forest Cottages and Forest Lodge etc.

In Station Road (south end), several large Victorian houses have been built, including Winston House, Carlton Villa, Westbourne and Eastfield Lodge. Adjacent to the latter house in Station Approach stands a terrace of houses. Just to give an idea of the inhabitants of the period, it is recorded in the 1891 Census, that at 'The Poplars', Station Approach, lived Robert Howard (aged 30) a leather factor's assistant, plus a cow-keeper and his wife, three cartmen and two female general servant domestics.

Moving down under the Railway Bridge towards St. Bartholomew's Church, Oakhurst Terrace stands out to the right, having been built about 1875. Several large terrace houses are situated at the lower end of Clifton Terrace along with Claremont Villas. Forest Hall shows little settlement, except for a few houses and shops near the station.

'The Hall' at Forest Hall (built 1690) covered in thick ivy, is very prominent and is the home of William Frederick Wilson, landowner. At the crossroads at Clousden Hill, stands a public house called 'The Three Tuns' (later the 'Clousden Hill Inn').

Bulmer's Directory of 1888 describes Forest Hall as a modern village of suburban residences, chiefly inhabited by gentlemen who have businesses in Newcastle. It has easy railway communication and is year by year increasing in size.

Turning into Great Lime Road and moving towards West Moor, we pass Dial Cottage - the home of both George Stephenson and his son Robert. Described as a hamlet in Bulmer's 1888 Directory, this township was chiefly inhabited by miners employed at the neighbouring collieries. The moor, which gives it a name, was used previous to its enclosure and cultivation in 1790, as a course for the Newcastle races. A large disused pit heap (now the site of an industrial

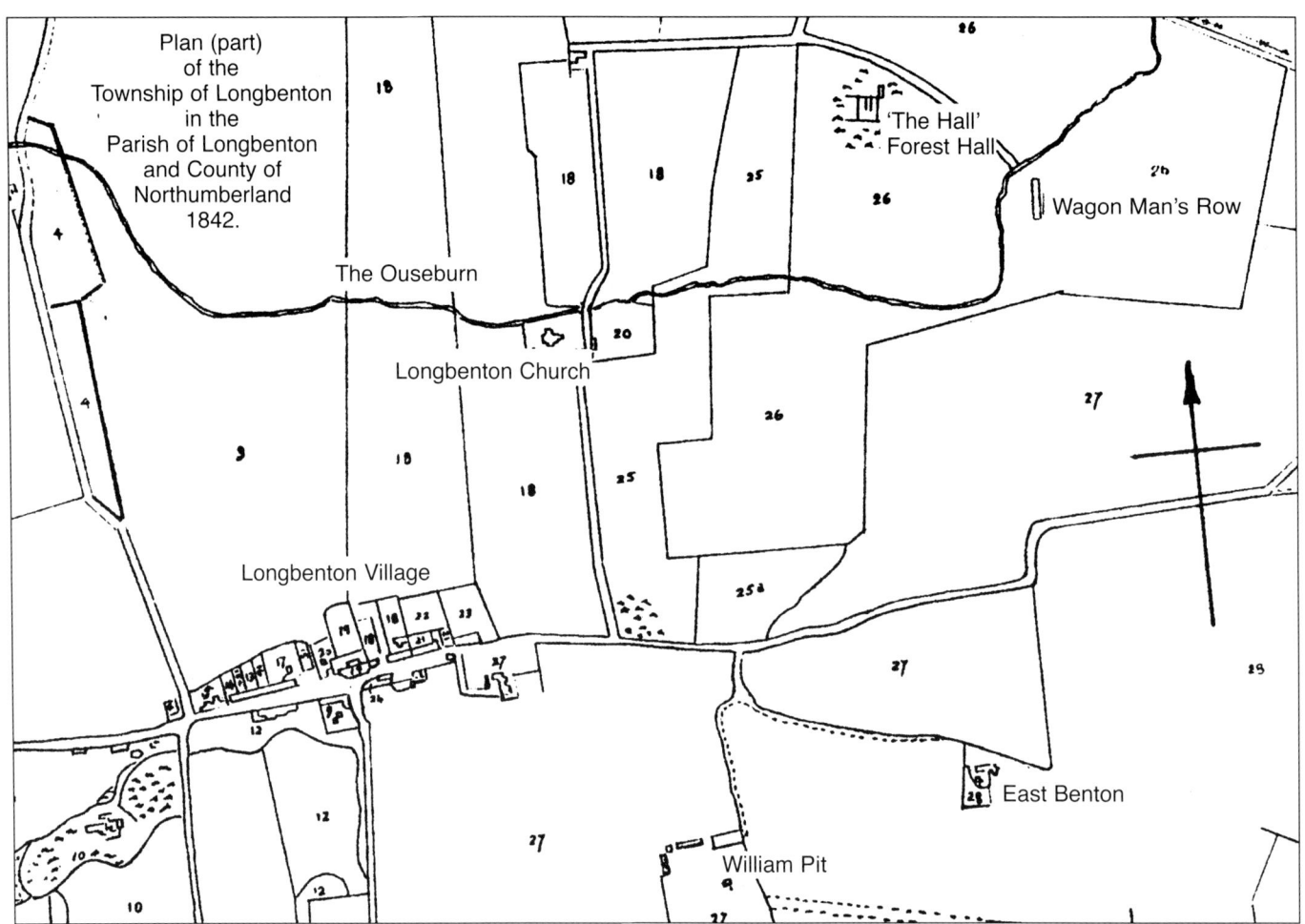

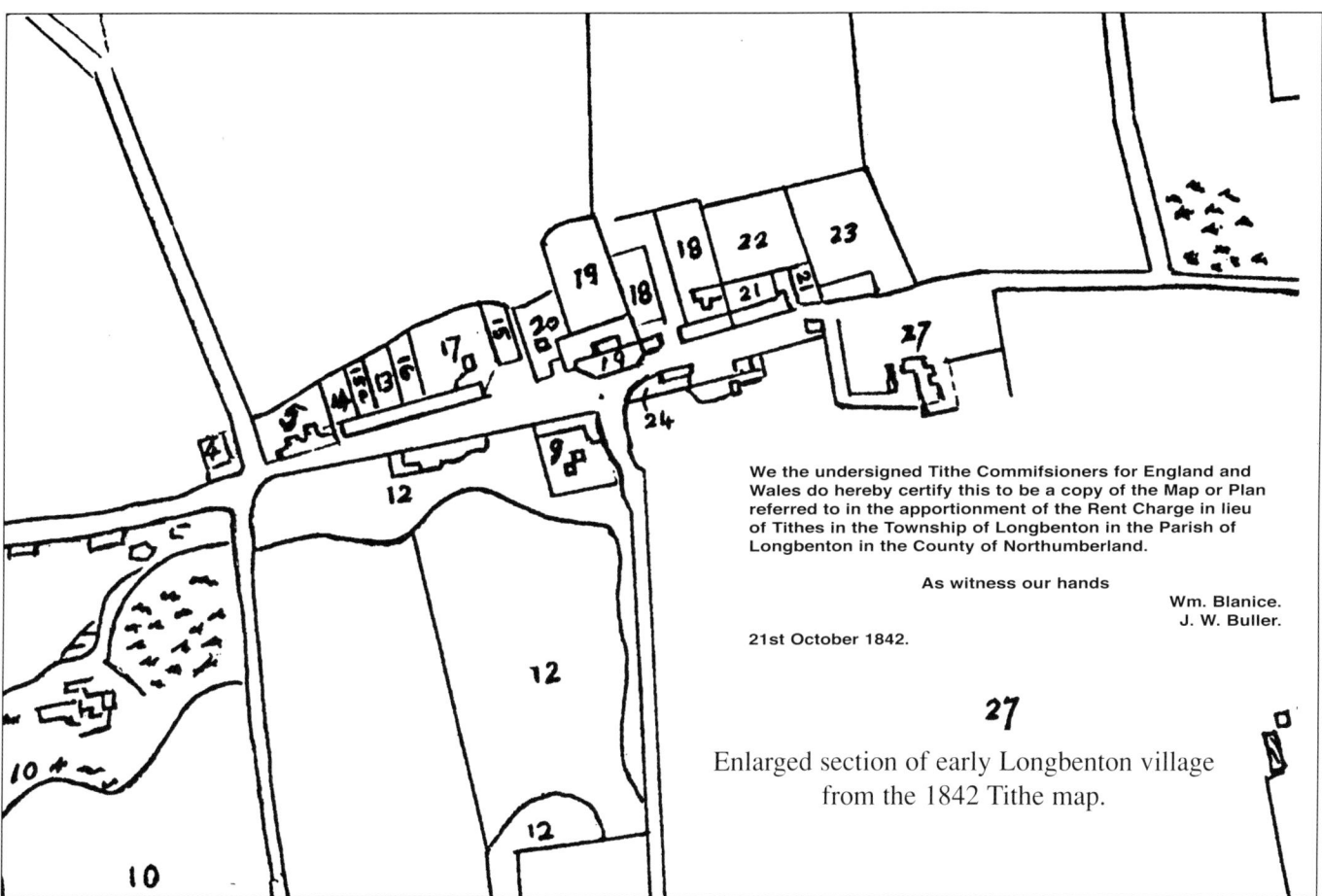

Enlarged section of early Longbenton village from the 1842 Tithe map.

The Landowners, Occupiers etc., as living in Longbenton Village in 1842

Landowners.	Occupiers.	Number on Plan.	Name and Description of Lands and Premises.
Bell Matthew	Robert Guy	25	Forest Hall.
	Revd. J. Besly	25a	Field at Longbenton.
Balliol College Master & Scholars of	John Hewison	9	Longbenton Farm.
Brandling Revd. Ralph Henry Trustees of	Thomas Morrow	4	House and land.
	William Boggor	22	A field at Benton.
	Revd. J. Besly	23	House and field/Benton.
	Matthew Forster	13	Cottages and gardens in Longbenton.
	Benjamin Hall and others.	21	Public House, 7 dwelling houses & garden ground.
Coulson Thomas	William Jowsey and others.	14	Public House, 4 dwellings and garden land, Longbenton
Craster T. W. Askew Craster.	John Gray	27	Benton Farm.
	Roger Bourne	28	East Benton Farm.
	Robert Potts	29	Rising Sun Farm.
	Roger Bourne & George Bold	16	House and gardens, Longbenton.

The Landowners, Occupiers etc., as living in Longbenton Village in 1842

Landowners.	Occupiers.	Number on Plan.	Name and Description of Lands and Premises.
Dixon Dixon Esq.	William Smith	10	Benton Hall and land.
	Mrs. Purvis Atkinson	12	Mansion House and land.
	Wm. Hewison	11	Benton Place Farm.
	Wm. Wrightson } H. Morrison } Jane Staig, } Ann Watson & } Ann Wood }	17	5 cottages & gardens.
	Wm. Robson	24	House, Blacksmith's shop and garden.
Hedley Robert Esq	Wm. Nesbit	18	Farm at Benton.
	Thos. Taylor	19	Mansion House & land.
Tyne Brewery The owners of	Wm. S. Boggor	15	Public House, dwelling house & garden grounds.
	John Duell	15a	Public House.
Wilson Frederick Wm.	Himself.	26	Forest Hall.
Glebe Land. Revd. J. Besly as Vicar.	W. Pringle	20	Farm and land

estate) marks the West Moor pit which 'died' in 1882 following a serious accident. The United Free Methodists, Primitive Methodists and Wesleyans each have chapels in the village and there is also a school which was erected some years ago by the owners of the colliery (the predecessor of the school which stands today).

Approaching Killingworth village by West Lane, we pass the church of St. John the Evangelist and then view several superior residences including Killingworth Hall and Killingworth House. Many gentlemen whose businesses are situated in Newcastle have their private houses here. Killingworth was separated from Longbenton and constituted a distinct ecclesiastical parish, by an Order in Council in 1865.

During the next few decades, a significant change takes place with a considerable amount of building in the area as wealth expands, chiefly due to industrialisation. Benton becomes more suburban with the development of many more Victorian / Edwardian semi-detached properties and terraces. Large semi-detached houses with gardens have appeared in The Grove and at the top end of Midhurst Road, while smaller terraced properties with backyards are being built, such as those in Sandringham Avenue, Beech Grove and Ashleigh Grove. (Ref. O.S.1913). The railways played an important role here, bringing trade to the region with the inevitable demand for shops and services.

The trams reached Forest Hall via. Longbenton in 1920 (followed by the trolleybuses) and thus this area became a popular residential area for those working in and around Newcastle.

The end of the Second World War brought even greater changes, when in the 1950's, the vast council housing estate was built at Longbenton. Later the main National Insurance complex was built nearby. Small industrial estates have appeared at Killingworth and Benton Square etc. and as this booklet is compiled, a very large industrial estate takes shape at Longbenton, aptly named 'Balliol'.

Several large housing estates have appeared (almost overnight) in the surrounding areas within the last two years, resulting in a considerable loss of both agricultural land and 'green-belt area'. With the storm clouds of unemployment locally, nationally and internationally, it remains to be seen as to whether this tremendous growth can be sustained.

WGE.   1999.

The Four Lane Ends, Longbenton, facing East. (Circa 1890). Benton Lane is to the left. Benton Road to the right. The Manor House, Front Street is prominent to the left, being early C.18 vernacular and now converted into C.20 flats.

The Four Lane Ends, Longbenton looking East, (Circa 1905). Hartley's workshop is on the immediate left. Benton Road to the right. A haystack can be seen in Rowell's farmyard. (The Manor House).
Note the road marks in the centre which suggests a move towards road widening.
In the distance, can be seen the cottages at Warden Place with gardens into the road.
The signpost reads: Killingworth Station 1.3/4, Gosforth Park 2, Cramlington 5.3/4, Shankhouse 7 and Newcastle Central Station 3.1/2.

Hartley's workshops at the Four Lane Ends, Longbenton in 1930 - looking North.

A Tilney family wedding photograph taken outside the home of Albert Tilney (Blacksmith), Forge House, Balliol Cottages, Front Street, Longbenton in 1904. The forge was situated at the rear of the premises. The house can be seen quite clearly at the far end of the second block of buildings on the next photograph (and as it is today).

Front Street, Longbenton viewed from the Four Lane Ends, facing East. (Circa 1920).
Looking left towards Balliol Cottages, Warden Place and the Sun Inn (re-named on the 21st November, 1995 as 'The Benton Ale House').
Note that the tramway has arrived, the trams having reached the Four Lane Ends in 1916.
Benton House (now the Conservative Club) can be seen middle right.

Front Street, Longbenton 1900. R. A. Smith (grocer) and his son Charles to the right. The Sun Inn (now The Benton Ale House) can be seen to the left.

The same view as in the previous photo, taken in 1905.
The grocer's shop has been rebuilt as 'Wanwood House'. This is South View as it stands today.
The Black Bull car park is immediately to the right.

A Famous Former Resident -

Thomas Addison M.D., F.R.C.P.

Educated at Rutter's School (the First Parish School which stood on the site now occupied by Pearson's Garage), the Royal Grammar School, Newcastle upon Tyne and the University of Edinburgh, reading Medicine. Appointed to Guy's Hospital, London about 1817, where he later became Senior Physician. Founder of the modern science of Endrocrinology and discoverer of Addison's Disease.
President of both the Westminster and Royal Medico-Chirurgical Societies.

Source:- The History of Longbenton Church of England School — D. J. Scott.
The Register of the Royal Grammar School.
Guy's Hospital Reports 1926.

Rear view of the house at Longbenton in which Thomas Addison (1793-1860) was born. This house and grocer's shop adjoined the 'old' Black Bull Inn.

The 'old' Black Bull, Front Street, Longbenton - 1926.
Note the insurance plaque on the wall.
A coaching house. The Vicar kept his horse in stables behind the inn.

The 'old' Black Bull, Front Street, Longbenton in 1936.
Peggy's Parlour (to the immediate left of the Inn) has now replaced the butcher's shop.
A single decker tram makes its slow journey down to the Forest Hall terminus.

Benton House, Hoylake Avenue, Longbenton - backing onto the South side of Front Street. (Circa 1910). Built 1740. The seat and estate of the Bigge family. William Bigge II, was appointed High Sheriff of Northumberland in 1750 and for three generations this was something of a family tradition. His son, Thomas Charles (born 1739) was High Sheriff in 1771 as was his son Charles William in 1802. In 1908, Benton House became the home of the Benton Golf Club and following the disappearance of the course under a large housing estate, the house became the property of the Benton Conservative Club in 1949.

Longbenton Mission Room, Front Street, Longbenton (Circa 1886).
The cottage was one of a row, almost opposite the old vicarage (site now in flats). Open air meetings were originally held in 'Barrack Square' at the top of Coach Lane. These meetings were so successful that a cottage was acquired as a Mission Room, where services were held between 1886-1905.
The Mission Room was the predecessor of Benton Methodist Church.

Longbenton Church Vicarage, Front Street. Built c. 1734 for Charles Hayton (Vicar 1734-1743). Once known as North House. A large rambling house, with ample accommodation for official visitors, such as Archdeacons or perhaps the Bishop who would travel with his chaplain and other staff. Since 1944 it has been owned by the University of Newcastle upon Tyne.

The Coach Lane to Little Benton and Walker was opposite the Vicarage and the Toll Gate was situated at the North end. It cost a penny to use the road and three pence for carts.

'Lost' Mansions.

As we progress down through Longbenton, we must mention three large mansions that have long since disappeared.

First, we list Benton Lodge, a large Victorian residence that stood near the junction of Benton Lodge Avenue and Thropton Avenue, having very extensive grounds. The lodge to the estate stood on the West side of Benton Road, almost in the centre of where the present shopping complex is situated. Once occupied by the Smiths of Smith Dock (who later moved across the road into the Bigge's old house). In 1887, it was occupied by Miss Elizabeth Anderson and later by an accountant, Alfred Carr. Earlier this century, it was occupied by Sir Neville and Lady Hadcock.

At the South end of Coach Lane, on either side of the present Red Hall Drive, stood two large mansions, Benton Hall to the East and Benton Park to the West.

Benton Hall (sometimes known as Little Benton Hall and occasionally as Benton White House while Mackenzie in 1825 referred to it as Benton House) - lay North and West respectively of the present Coast Road and Red Hall Drive - in the vicinity of where the Lochside Public House now stands. It was built in 1760 (the wings may have been added later) by Thomas Bigge, a coal-owner and brother of William. In 1838, it was the residence of Mrs. James Anderson and after 1858, the estate was converted into a public Botanical Garden.

Benton Park was sited adjacent to that of Benton Hall i.e. on the latter's western side, bounded by the present Coast Road, Etherstone Avenue and Red Hall Drive. Built in the late eighteenth century, it had projecting wings, linked to the main block by curving walls or arcades. Dixon Brown owned it and later Dixon Dixon of Longbenton and occupied by the former's son-in-law, William Clark of Belford Hall, for whom Dobson surveyed the estate in 1813. At one time it was known as Red Hall and at another time, Benton Park Hall - and as can be seen from previous notes, the tracing of these mansions has been very confusing over the years, due to the occasional change of names.

In 1838, Benton Park was the residence of John Potts, a coal-owner and later by Edward Potts. By 1871, it was owned by Edward Liddell (1815-79), formerly of Jesmond Park and it remained in the possession of the Liddells until 1897. Benton Park was finally demolished during the 1930's to make way for residential development.

It is interesting to note that the lodges of all three of the respective mansions listed here, were situated at the north end of the estates, which appears to indicate that the main approach to them was via. Longbenton Village.

- - - - - - - - - - - - - - - -

Reference:- Lost Houses of Newcastle and Northumberland by Thomas Faulkner and Phoebe Lowery.

North House, Front Street, Longbenton.
A good later C.18 house (altered in the C.19) of five bays and two storeys, with two-bay wings on the left and right. Doorway with broken pediment on attached Tuscan columns. At present, owned by the University of Newcastle upon Tyne. Carl Igl (an Austrian inventor) lived here before he moved to Killingworth House. (Fuller details given later).

Longbenton National School, Front Street, Longbenton looking towards the Four Lane Ends. (Circa 1880).
Nine years later in 1889, an extension was built at the East end of the school to ease overcrowding.

Front Street, Longbenton. (Circa 1899).
The 'old' Ship Inn is seen to the left and Longbenton National School (built 1871) on the right. The school was demolished in 1973, as a new school, re-named Longbenton Church of England Aided First School, had been built adjacent.
A full account of the school can be found in 'The History of Longbenton Church of England School' by D. J. Scott.

Front Street, Longbenton, (pre 1916). Miss Mary Burdus's sweet shop (opposite the school). Miss Burdus was well known for her voluntary action in ushering children over the road, in the mornings, lunchtime and following afternoon school. Anderson Cottages, the 'old' Ship Inn (in flats) and the new Ship Inn.

The 'old' Ship Inn, Front Street, Longbenton. (Circa 1890).

Front Street, Longbenton - looking West - about 1910. The Church School is on the left behind the trees. The 'new' Ship Inn is on the right. (Built 1904).

The Old School House (Rutter's School) and Stackyard Lonnen, Benton, in 1791.
It stood on the site now occupied by Pearson's Garage, opposite the Ship Inn.
(from an old engraving).

Front Street, Longbenton (Circa 1905). Both 'old' and 'new' Ship Inns are seen in the centre. Entrance on left leads to Benton Farm.

The William Pit (known in later years as the 'Billy Pit')

The site of this pit lay just to the East of the new National Benefits Agency (known as Tyneview Park) ie. at the lower end of the sports complex (Darsley Park) which is situated south of the junction of Station Road and Whitley Road. (position shown on the map on page 43).

This pit, along with nineteen cottages, started life around 1806, the pit being just one in a chain that belonged to Willington Colliery. The pit was 'worked-out' by 1843 but the colliery retained ownership of the cottages until about 1856, when the whole of the Willington Colliery was abandoned. The cottages were put up for auction at about this time but the subsequent owner or owners are unknown. The cottages remained in use until 1940, when they were finally demolished.

Details:

    Commencement: Shaft sunk / cottages built / work commenced between Jan. 1807 and Sept. 1808.

    The name William: Possibly named after William Brown (Co-owner of the Willington Colliery).

    Workforce: Most likely an average of 45 men and boys.

    Dimensions: Depth of shaft: 84 fathoms (504 ft).

    Name change: William to Billy; over a period of 18 years. (The Census Enumerator's Returns of 1861 mention the William Pit cottages and by the time of the 1871 Returns, the name had changed to Billy Pit).

The old pit shaft of the William Pit.

One of the 19 cottages (in two rows) at the William Pit site.

Children enjoying themselves at Benton Square (Circa 1895) - in similar circumstances to those at Billy Pit. A pit cottage consisted of two rooms and a pantry, the rooms being paved with bricks. Above, was an open attic unceiled with access by loft ladder. The upstairs bed (or beds) was by necessity on the floor.

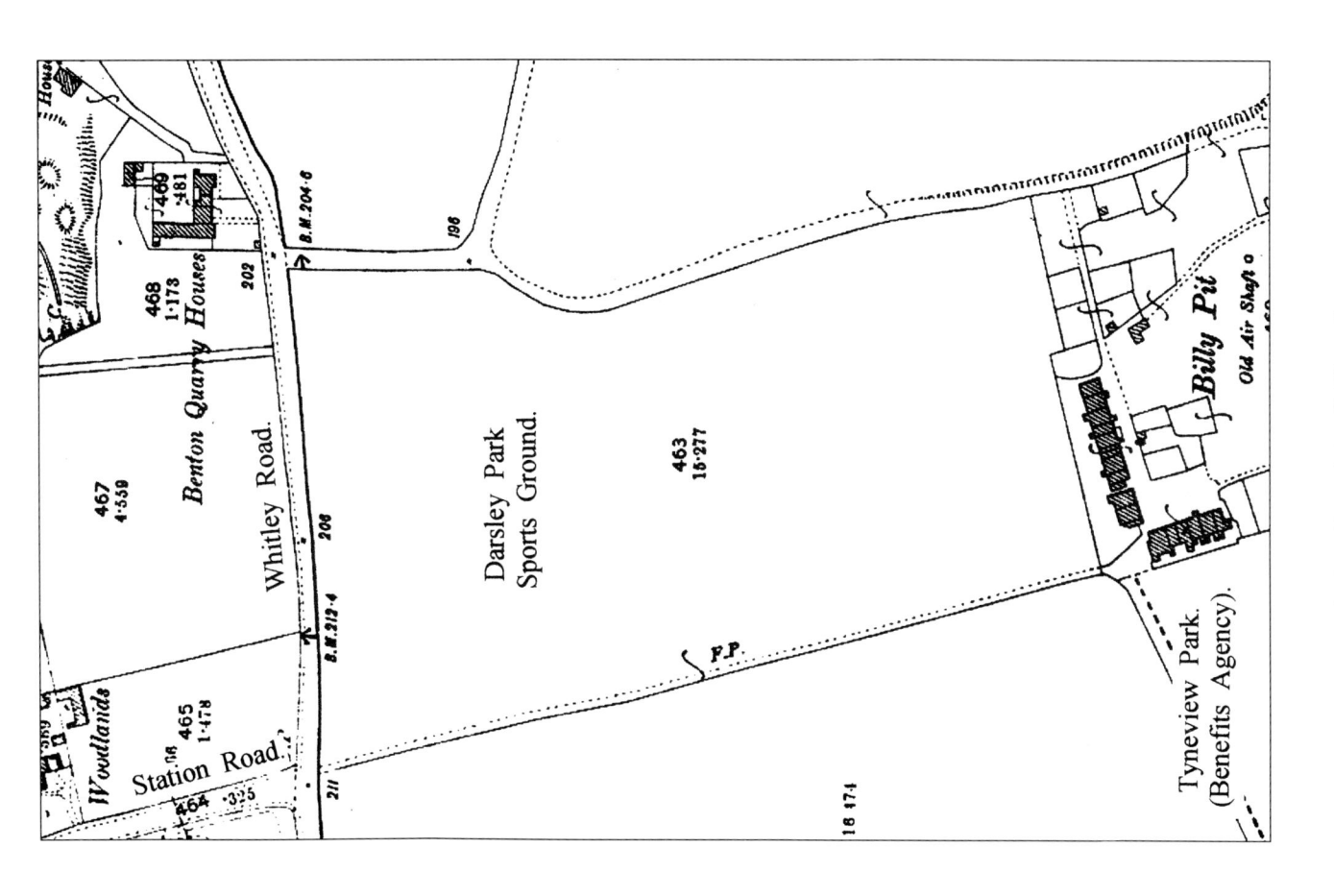

Site of Billy Pit and the Colliery Cottages.
Ref: 2nd Edition O.S. 1894.

A tram car in 1946, turning from Station Road, Benton into Whitley Road. The trams reached to the
Forest Hall terminus in 1921 (the terminus being situated just south of Forest Hall railway station).
At intervals along the single tramtrack, you would find several places where a double track was provided
(seen clearly in this photograph). This was to allow a tram to wait and allow an oncoming tram to pass safely.

Station Road, Benton looking North (1920-25).
Tram 73, Gosforth Park via. New Market Street (Front exit car), reaches the top of the bank.
Station Approach lies to the left and Thornhill Road to the right. Note the cobbled entrance to 'Norwood'
in the right foreground.

The Grove, Benton. (Circa 1905).
These large Victorian houses were built in 1895. This road has an unusual feature, in that the sycamore trees grow in the road rather than on the pavement.

Railway Stations in the Longbenton, Benton and Forest Hall areas.

The exact positions of the railway stations serving both Benton and Forest Hall over the last 150 years, can be very confusing (to say the least) when researched, so the following details are recorded here as a matter of historical interest.

Benton Station — opened on the present site of 'old' Forest Hall station (i.e. on the Newcastle and Berwick line) on the 1st March 1847. This station was renamed Forest Hall (NER line) on 1st December 1874 and finally closed on 15th September 1958.

Longbenton Station — (or sometimes referred to as Benton Station e.g. Bradshaw Sept. 1864 and now and again in the Blyth and Tyne timetables for 1864 and 1865 - hence the confusion) opened on the site of the present Four Lane Ends Metro station on 27th June 1864 and closed on 1st March 1871.
The new station Four Lane Ends, opened on 11th March 1980 (Tyne & Wear PTE).

Forest Hall Station — opened at Wagon Man's Row (on the north side of the present Metro line near where a footpath passes under the railway. Once the site of Benton East Junction signal box) - it opened on 27th June 1864 and closed on 1st March 1871. (Blyth and Tyne railway line). (Please refer to the 1842 Tythe map on page 12 to see the exact position of Wagon Man's Row).

Benton Station — opened on its present site on 1st March 1871 (Blyth and Tyne railway) and closed on 23rd January 1978 (British Rail).
Reopened on 11th August 1980 (Tyne and Wear PTE).

100-2-71.

BLYTH AND TYNE RAILWAY.

ON AND AFTER

MARCH 1ST,

THE FOLLOWING

ALTERATIONS

TO THE

TRAIN SERVICE

OF THIS COMPANY WILL TAKE EFFECT:—

TYNEMOUTH BRANCH

SUNDAYS.—The Trains now leaving Newcastle at 7·45 p.m., and Tynemouth at 8·30 p.m., will leave at 8·0 & 8·45 p.m respectively.

The NEW STATION at BENTON will be opened out on the 1st of March, 1871, and the Stations at LONG BENTON and FOREST HALL will be closed for traffic.

☞ FOR FURTHER PARTICULARS SEE THE COMPANY'S TIME TABLES.

Benton Station, looking East. (Circa 1905).
The first public electric train left New Bridge Street station for Benton on Tuesday, 29th March, 1904. This was the first electric train to be operated by any British main line railway company.
Seen here is a typical electric train of the period.
At Benton, a gantry of signals was erected in readiness for the curve to join the main line south of Forest Hall, but this was not built at that time and, as will be seen, the left-hand arms are 'crossed' out of use. The line straight ahead was - and still is - to Monkseaton and Tynemouth, with the curve on the right down to the main line at Benton Quarry. The north-west curve was eventually installed in World War 2 and in an emergency allowed trains from Scotland to reach Central Station via the old Blyth and Tyne line through South Gosforth, Jesmond and Manors North.

Oakhurst Terrace, Benton. (Circa 1900). Viewed from Benton Station platform (south side). These houses were built about 1875.

Station Road, Benton looking South. (Circa 1905).

Station Road, Benton looking South. (Circa 1910).
J. L. Long's newsagency shop can be seen at the top of the ramp. (J. L. Long was the father of the late Gordon Long, local historian and manager of Lloyd's Bank, Forest Hall for many years). Note the sloping footpaths on either side of the railway bridge which remained until the traffic increased in the middle 40's.

Benton Methodist Church, Station Road, Benton.
Built during 1904 and the official Opening Service took place on Wednesday, 1st February, 1905. These new premises became the first public building in the district to have electricity installed. On Saturday, 25th September, 1937 a new Hall was opened which had been built on the North side of the church. On 30th November, 1957, the 'Liddell Hall' was opened (sited on the South side of the church) - having been given in loving memory of their parents, by the son and daughters of Mark and Susannah Liddell.

Station Road, Benton looking South towards Benton Station railway Bridge. (Circa 1900).

St. Bartholomew's Parish Church, Benton. (Circa 1920). Rebuilt 1791 by William Newton. Originally dedicated to St. Andrew in 820 A.D. The church is of particular interest for its early Gothic revival tower and spire, a well proportioned composition of 1790. The later Victorian Gothic work, 'lancet' in the chapel and 'perpendicular' in the south aisle with its attractive porch, is pleasing work of its period. The specious interior contains a font of 1857 with floral and heraldic carving, an interesting series of mural tablets, and two of the earliest ledger stones in the county, one dated 1581 to John Fenwick and the other to John Killingworth and his family 1587-1720. A stained glass East window was given by Dr. Thomas Addison of Spring Gardens, London as a memorial to his parents.

Longbenton Church 'old' Parish Hall, Station Road, Benton. Opened in 1925.
Replaced by new housing when the New Hall was built on the North side of the church.

The Assembly Rooms, Station Road, Forest Hall. (Circa 1910). Later the Embassy Ballroom, destroyed by fire in 1963. Fir Tree Walk (a popular walk at the time) lies to the left. Site of the Percy Hedley School in the centre.
The Ouseburn, which runs under the road in the foreground and is shown clearly on the 1842 Tithe map on page 12 is traditionally the boundary between Benton and Forest Hall. This boundary has 'disappeared' in recent years, as the GPO now classes the whole area as Forest Hall NE12.

Station Road, Forest Hall, looking North towards Forest Hall station. (Circa 1910).
Lloyds Bank (now closed) can be seen in the foreground.

Forest Hall NER railway station crossing gates. (Circa 1910).

Forest Hall NER railway station. (Circa 1910). A train, travelling north, approaches the south platform.

Front Street, Forest Hall. (Circa 1910). Durey's general shop.

South View, Station Road, Forest Hall. (Circa 1890). Looking towards Forest Hall railway station.

The Presbyterian Church, Station Road, Forest Hall. Now known as Christ Church (URC). (Circa 1900). Built 1886.

Garget's cycle and gramophone store. (Circa 1920). This store, with a smithy adjoining, was situated on the corner of the junction between Station Road North and Forest Hall Road.

The driveway leading to the Hall, Forest Hall, which commenced at the junction of Park Drive and Westcroft Road. A large air-raid shelter was erected underground during World War 2, just to the right of this photo.

The Hall, Forest Hall. (Circa 1900). Built 1690.
Forest Hall gave its name to the suburb now occupying the area of its very extensive estate. The Western portion of the Hall (seen to the left) incorporated part of the original medieval tower, although the crenellations were modern. Richard Wilson (1695-1759) was probably responsible for building the five-bay central block, the Eastern wing being a later addition. During the 19th century, the Hall was frequently tenanted (e.g. in 1834 to John Straker, a coal-owner). The Wilsons re-occupied it c. 1910-56.
The Hall was demolished in the early 1960's to make way for the building of Woodside Court, off Westcroft Road.

Clousden Hill, Forest Hall - looking North. (Circa 1900). The horse-trough was removed shortly after this photo was taken and re-appeared at the side of the road, planted with flowers in 1984.

Willow Bridge, Great Lime Road, Forest Hall looking West. (Circa 1905).

Letchwell Cottage, off Great Lime Road, West Moor. (Circa 1895).
Mr. Cherry and his son in their trap. Note the Laburnum Arch.

A Famous Former Resident -
Robert Stephenson, M.P., D.C.L., M.Inst.C.E.
President, Institute of Civil Engineers.

Son of George, the famous engine-wright at West Moor Colliery, was educated at Longbenton Parish School (1809 - 1815), Dr. Bruce's School, Newcastle upon Tyne and then attended the University of Edinburgh for a session.
In 1822, he returned from Edinburgh and commenced his apprenticeship to engineering, under his father, who had established a steam-engine factory at Newcastle. Working together and continuously improving the technology involved, the Newcastle factory became the largest and most famous in the world, producing some one thousand engines. Many of these went to all the countries of Europe and to the United States. A writer in 1850, said, while speaking of the achievements of railway enterprise, especially under the auspices of Mr. Stephenson, that we then had about 5,000 miles of railway in the construction of which 250,000,000 cubic yards, or not less than 350,000,000 tons of earth and rock had, in tunnel, embankment and cutting, been moved.

Source: Microsoft Encarta 98 De Luxe.
         The History of Longbenton Church of England School - D. J. Scott.

Dial Cottage, Great Lime Road, West Moor. (Circa 1895).
The West Moor pit-head is seen to the left. An unremarkable late C. 18 or early C. 19 rubble and pantiled cottage with additions, which would be merely a pleasant vernacular survival in a sea of ribbon development, if it had not been the home from 1803-1815, of George Stephenson and his son Robert. Together, while Robert was a schoolboy, they made the sundial over the door, dated 11th August, 1816. (Photograph overleaf).

The sundial at Dial Cottage, Great Lime Road, Killingworth.
The plaque gives details of George Stephenson's life and work during his time at Killingworth.

1893 - 1993
100 years of Education

Wilma House (in the foreground), Great Lime Road, West Moor. Previously the new Connexion Church (building began 1888). Later joined by the United Free Methodists (in about 1907) and the Primitive Methodists in 1925. West Moor school can be seen behind (now West Moor First School) built in 1893. The original school building was situated in the Miners' welfare building at the north end of the terraces of pit houses.

The West Moor Pit Head

    In 1805, the first shaft of the West Moor pit was sunk - just north of Great Lime Road and to the East of the main NER railway bridge (as it is now). The miners' houses were nearby in Long Row, Short Row, Lane Row, Cross Row, Crank Row, High Row, Paradise Row and Office Row (formerly Quality Row).
(The exact position of these houses can be seen on the map of West Moor on the following page).
    In 1810, the sinking of the High Pit on the high ground east of Killingworth village was commenced.
    In 1819, Killingworth was the world's deepest coal mine at 1,200 feet and by 1822, it was probably the most technically advanced.

    Killingworth, or West Moor Colliery as it came to be called at the end of its days, was one of the pits sending coal down waggonways to the Tyne to be shipped to London. Both pits closed in 1882 following a serious accident.

    The full history of these pits can be found in 'How long did the ponies live? The Story of the Colliery of Killingworth and West Moor' by Roy Thompson.

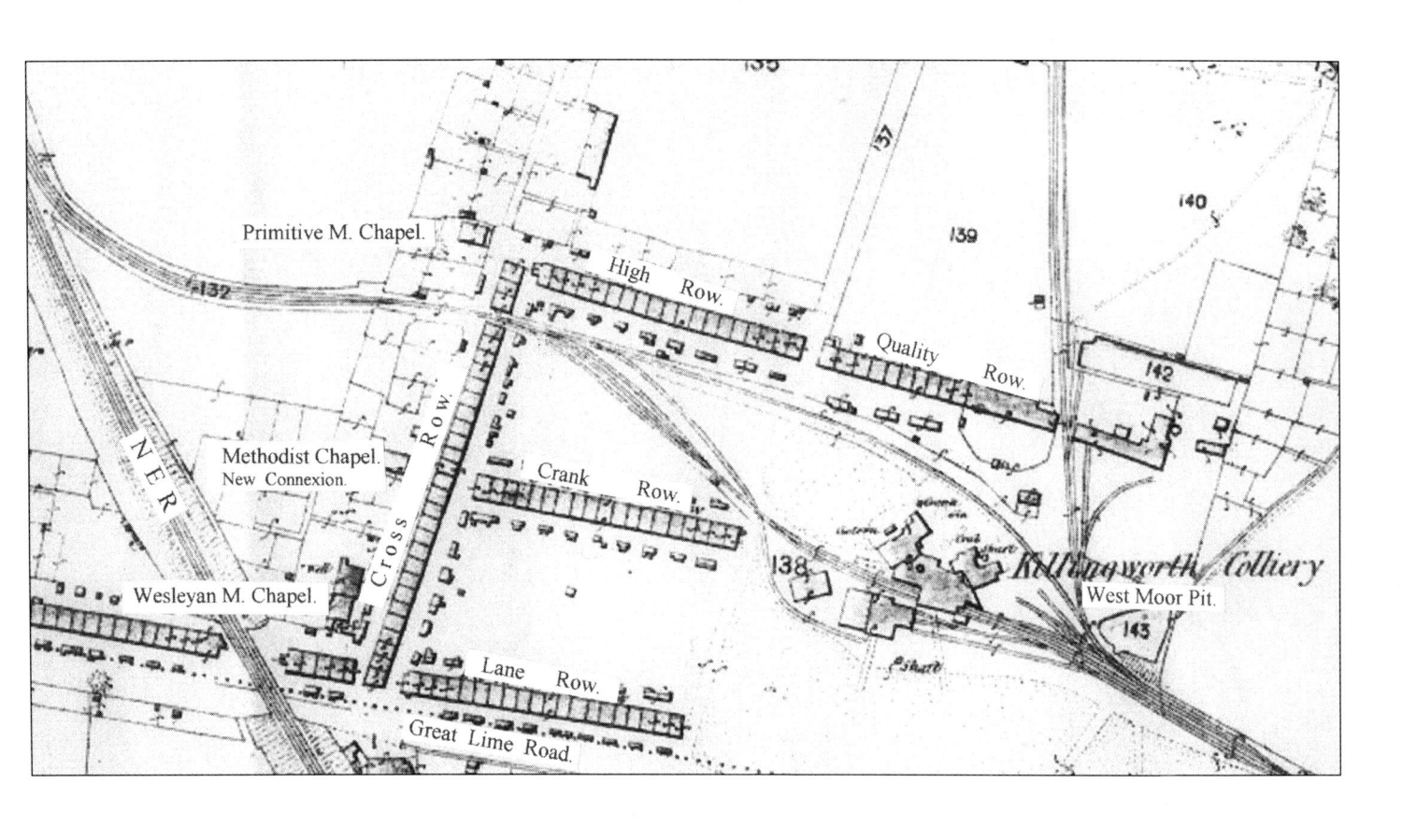

Site of the West Moor Pit and Colliery Cottages.
Ref: 1st Edition O.S. 1858.

Crank Row, West Moor looking East with the West Moor pit head in the distance (1900 - 1905).

First Shop, Great Lime Road, West Moor. (Circa 1857).
This shop and cottages were sited immediately adjacent to the bridge carrying the NER railway line.

Kenilworth House, Westmoor. (Circa 1904).
This was the Post Office and was situated on Great Lime Road, just West of the George Stephenson Inn.
At the door stands Robert Henderson (Postman) and his daughter.

St. John the Evangelist Church, Killingworth by E. Bassett Keeling. (Circa 1910).
Consecrated in 1869. Viewed from the south-west corner of the churchyard.
No tower, no bell-cote. Built of stones of deliberately varied colours and with bands of red sandstone.
On the buttresses, the crescent emblem of the Dukes of Northumberland.

Killingworth Village, looking West towards the church (Circa 1900). North Farm (built 1725) stands out to the right and is the oldest village building, being a typical modest farmhouse. Dated on the lintel 1725 DP (Deborah Potts). Its solid sandstone foundation can be seen at the base of the steps which lead up to the House.

The Plough Inn, Killingworth village, which was rebuilt in 1910. (Seen here about 1920).
Killingworth Hall can be seen in the centre.

Killingworth village, looking East. (Circa 1903).
North Farm is seen to the left. Plough Row is in the foreground on the right, with the Plough Inn behind.

Killingworth village, looking West towards the church. (Circa 1900).
Killingworth Hall can be seen to the left.

Killingworth Hall (home of the Killingworth family). Rebuilt 1765.
A C. 18 Georgian Mansion, designed by Lancelot Coxon and stands in over 2 acres of magnificent grounds.

Killingworth House (Circa 1898). An 18th century Georgian Mansion. Designed by Lancelot Coxon. The former property of Admiral Robert Roddam and where he died in 1843. Later, the home of the General Manager of the West Moor Pit. Another resident was Carl Igl, who came to the area from Austria in 1924. A profuse inventor, his biggest commercial success being an antiseptic called 'Iglodine'. The two castleated houses opposite are also attributed to Igl's invention - said to be the first concrete buildings in the country. Killingworth house was demolished in 1956.

Killingworth Cottage (Circa 1930) - the residence of the Punshon family, who were associated with it for at least 300 years.

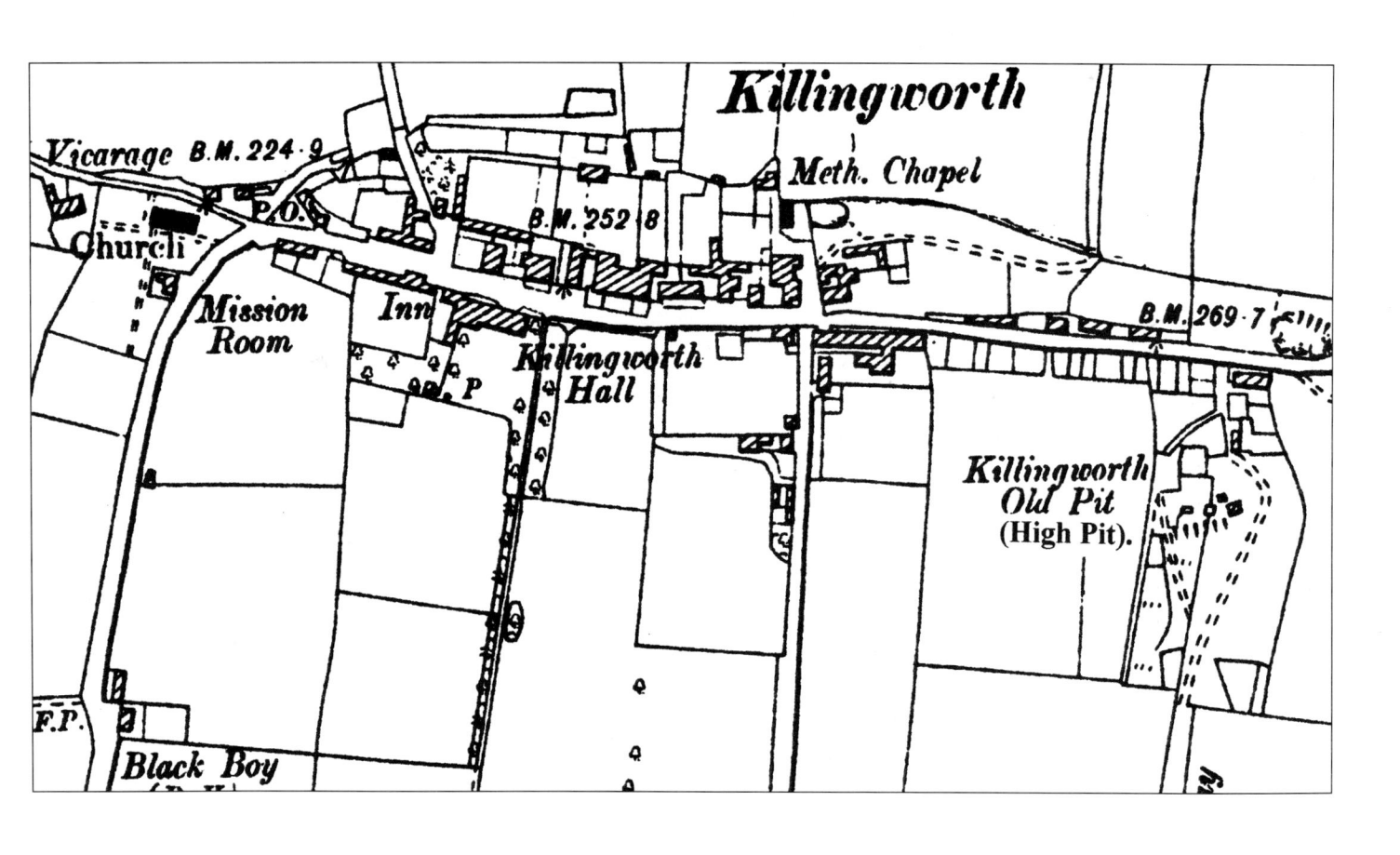

Killingworth Village.
Ref: 2nd Edition O.S. 1894.

JAMES WEIGHTMAN,

Cartwright, &c.

KILLINGWORTH,

RESPECTFULLY begs Leave to inform his Friends, and the Public in general, that he has got a

HEARSE,

WHICH HE INTENDS TO

LET OUT FOR HIRE,

Either with or without a Horse.

Killingworth, Oct. 7, 1817.   Newcastle: MARSHALL, Printer.